I0625466

UNLOCK THE MIND

BY STIMULATING
THE GOD FORCE
WITHIN

P. Augusta D.

ARPress
ILLUMINATING IDEAS,
EMPOWERING VOICES

ARPress
45 Dan Road Suite 36
Canton MA 02021
Hotline: 1(800) 220-7660
Fax: 1(855) 752-6001

Ordering Information:
Quantity Sales. Special discounts are available on quantity purchases by corporations, associations, and others. For details, contact the publisher at the address above.

Printed in the United States of America.

ISBN-13	Paperback	979-8-89389-074-7
	eBook	979-8-89389-075-4

Library of Congress Control Number: 2024912903

CONTENT

PREFACE

Because of the way the world is evolving, the Human Being has to make a decision, *is the race going to continue to partake of other men's sins or is the race going to partake of the benefit?* Very few Humans know what the benefit is because the smartest Human is only using ten percent of Human Potential. The reason Human Potential is so low, the *Homo Sapien* does not focus on what the Creator God instilled within the body of the Human Being. I call this the Potential God Force Within and every Human has this force—it just has to be stimulated. The focus of this book is to help you develop this Force and open your mind to the ninety percent we are not using. The Bible mentions renewing of the mind, this suggest to me that there is part of the brain that needs stimulation. I believe this part is the Alpha Brain Wave. I also believe that the ninety percent Human Potential we are not using is stored in the Alpha Brain Wave. The Alpha Brain Wave is the dominant brain wave of every human being from birth until eight years old. This is the brain wave that keeps us focused on being human. At eight years old the *Homo Sapien* becomes interested in the world around them and the Alpha Brain Wave becomes dormant. The Alpha Brain Wave is still in the mind, it has to be stimulated to make it active. I show you a very simple body movement that stimulates the Alpha Wave making it active; this movement is done before getting out of bed. You will learn how to breathe, how to direct breathing to where you want it to go and how oxygen is so important in keeping the organs in your body healthy. This book focuses on four body movements that are done before getting out of bed. These movements help to stimulate the God Force within.

INTRODUCTION

Unlock the God force within; it is my belief that most human beings are looking for more pleasure and less frustration out of life. People are looking for a guide to help them live the good life. Everything you need to live the good life you were born with. The guide you are looking for is the God Force Within. The *homo sapien* has always been told that we are made in the image of God, but we have to realize that the image is not a mirror image; but specific God like powers that are internal. When we learn how to use these powers, we have tapped into the God Force Within. To trigger the God Force Within you have to believe in yourself. But first you have to have faith; faith in yourself that the Kingdom of God is within you. The God Force within is contained in our internal system. The key to this system is our brain and what makes the brain function properly is oxygen. All of our internal organs need oxygen, so the first thing you will learn from this guide is how to oxygenate your body, focus on the natural way of doing things and using only what you were born with to stimulate the God Force Within. . You need no equipment other than your body and believing in yourself as a human being. The human being is so amazing that we had to be created; because we have a likeness that is so different from anything else on earth. The human body is kinetic, everything is connected. When one system is working badly the other systems tend to work badly, but when one system is working properly the other systems tend to work properly. The Kingdom of God is about working properly; so let's seek the Kingdom of God.

CHAPTER 1

We are made of and possess God like qualities, and we have the right and ability to develop and use them. Where are these God-like qualities? Within us. What is the meaning of the statement; The Kingdom of God is within you? It means that as human beings (God's Greatest Creation) our strength is internal. We have to stimulate our systems positively, and the God like qualities will shine through. Everything we need to stimulate our internal systems we were born with. When we get a glimpse of the true nature of the God power within us and use it, the results are truly amazing. You control your own good and may transform your life into an experience of happiness, health and prosperity. You have to realize that it is through law of nature that the body is built and maintained. It is constantly at work sustaining God's perfect idea of humankind. It keeps us breathing, because oxygen is the key to life. What was the human being before God blew oxygen into the body; just a lump of clay. Once oxygen was introduced to the lump of clay it became a living being. The first step in keeping the marvelously intricate machinery of the body in operation is knowing how to breathe. Yes we go through the motion of taking oxygen into our bodies because it is an involuntary function.

Breathing is directing this function so that the whole body gets proper oxygen. We have to create an atmosphere and tone of the body that can be considered as wholesome, happy, optimistic and therefore healthy. Breathing fully filling the lungs with oxygen, ensuring that the brain gets enough oxygen. Fifty percent of the oxygen we take into our bodies has to be used by the brain; but the rest of the body's organs need oxygen also. If you focus on this fact it will help you remember to keep plenty of oxygen in the body. How do you keep plenty of oxygen in the body? By oxygenating the blood. When we understand there is a definite law with which we are working, it is much easier to have faith in yourselves to know that you have within you what is required for healing.

CHAPTER 2

The law of directing of the breath is misunderstood and literally ignored in today's society. The human being has the ability to control your breathing; to direct the breath where you want it to go. The Creator gave the human being the power to control the most important life-giving force in this world, oxygen and today's society ignores this law. The process of change requires the re-education of your body to respond positively to the directing of the breath. There is no limit to the good that can manifest through the proper use of the breath. As human beings we have to understand the nature of the unseen part of our Universe and the way it works; whole heartedly believe in it, then we can effectively use it; to control breath is to control life force and perhaps life itself. Breath control contains tremendous potential for remarkable healing and invigorating powers. In some countries geriatricians now advocate regular breathing exercises as a means of prolonging life. Oxygenation of the blood, by filling the lungs with oxygen, the oxygenation of the stream is improved, every vital organ, endocrine gland, nervous center and body tissue receive better nourishment. When inhaling push the stomach out, inflating it like a balloon until you feel it in your chest; inhale through your nose;

once you have filled the lungs with oxygen; form an O with your lips and exhale through your mouth, pulling the stomach in resulting in complete emptying of the lungs. When exhaling, the breath can be directed to any part of the body by will power and concentration, thus contributing to physical well-being; controlled breath is used for self-healing. Learn how to use the life force in oxygen by concentration; to breathe correctly is to stay young longer, your breathing slows down; slowing the breath down rests the heart, pacifies the nerves and relaxes the whole system. When this type of breathing is mastered, the ability to concentrate is developed, you have established rhythmical breathing, thus creating more balance in your body. You think more effectively, able to affirm more positively what you need so that your life becomes wholesome, fine, successful and good.

CHAPTER 3

O ne must clearly realize that there is no separation between the human being and God. When you learn breath control and how to direct your breathing, you become increasingly aware of your oneness with God. God intended humans to improve this earth and in doing so, to build into our own life the beauty of holiness. The human being has not only ruined the earth but destroyed our own health by wrong living and perversion of our own spiritual character. The two things that distinguish the human being from all other life is our ability to reason and adapt. The human being has been reasoning wrong; therefore we've become maladaptive. **Why does the human reason wrong? Because human beings have no faith in themselves.** We do a lot of proclaiming of faith, but our actions tell another story. The human being does not work with their faith and faith without works is dead. The human being has developed a lot of bad habits, mainly because we do not comply with the law of Cosmic Habit Force. Cosmic Habit Force is one universal principle through which order and harmony are carried out. It is a power that is equally available to the weak, strong, rich, poor, sick and well; it is said that learning to use the law of Cosmic Habit Force can provide the solution to all human problems. As human beings we have to condition our mind to receive this law. You have to know that your body is the house in which God dwells, that God is in you as you and what you are. You have to develop the habit that twice a day you will get as comfortable as you can, releasing all tension and at least for a few minutes forget the bodily discomfort, pain or any other symptom which distresses you. Try to relax all over, so that all tenseness disappears from your body. Remember, that your body is the house in which God dwells and convince yourself of your natural perfection.

CHAPTER 4

Research has found that the best times to relax yourself is in the morning when you awaken and at night before you go to sleep. Knowing how to breathe correctly can connect us to our natural perfection. Stretching· is a thing to do when you wake up every morning; you directly improve blood flow and speed delivery of oxygen and nutrients to the entire body. The *homo sapien* is both a spiritual being and a physical being. Learn to center ourselves so the spiritual and physical work together to decrease the stress in our lives. You will learn stretches that realign the more elusive innards such as the nervous, immune and glandular systems. The powerful combination of stretching routine of gentle postures promote a stronger mind/body connection. This is an inward practice that creates an internally fit body with emphasis on relaxation. Although, humans have always experienced stress, some think that the nature of current civilization and technology may be causing our tensions and anxieties to escalate at a rate faster than that of our ability to cope with them. To dispel this concern, moderate stretching on a regular basis brings a host of benefits including reducing the risk of depression and anxiety. The more often you stretch the more flexible and relaxed your muscles will become. By stretching, you can stimulate your internal organs and help keep your body stress resistant. If relaxation procedures are practiced with regularity, your level of tension and anxiety can be reduced significantly. Relaxation exercises increase our ability to tolerate stress and remain calm in the face of life's pressures and problems.

CHAPTER 5

T he first stretch is called the Alpha Stretch, it stimulates your 'Alpha Waves'. The human being contains more Alpha Waves than any other brain wave. From birth to eight years of age the human being operates in Alpha; kids will learn 25% more in their first eight years of life than they will as adults, because Alpha Brain Waves are the most active brain waves during the first eight years of life. After eight Beta Brain Waves become the most active for the majority of human beings and the *homo sapien* becomes aware of the world around them and the way our societies have developed causes the human being to stop focusing on their strength which is internal. The material world becomes the important part of human life and the God power within us becomes dormant. Once the *homo sapien* recognizes the God power within us, these powers can be stimulated and developed to be used the way the Creator intended they be used. By stimulating Alpha Brain Waves you increase awareness of yourself, body and mind. The Alpha Brain Wave state improves the human beings' natural abilities which are the God Force within you; such as self-healing to prevent illness, releasing the neurotransmitter serotonin that helps the *homo sapien* focus on pleasure instead of depression. Alpha Brain Waves are associated with a balanced mood and stable emotions, generated in a synchronized pattern between both right and left hemispheres of the brain. When the Alpha rhythm is established, your mind is balanced and in an optimal state of functioning; because our society has become more stressful since we entered the 21st century, it is important to find peace and contentment.

CHAPTER 6

P eace and contentment are built into the human psyche, all we have to do is know where to find it and how to stimulate it. The human beings' natural peace and contentment is found in the Alpha Brain Wave. Alpha is how the subconscious communicates with the conscious mind. A lot of important problems are solved in Alpha, because Alpha Brain Waves are for solving problems and improving creativity; our focus as human beings should be to stimulate the Alpha Brain Wave as soon as we wake up from sleep. The Alpha stretch is an excellent movement to stimulate Alpha Brain Waves. This movement is done when you wake up from sleep. Lie in bed flat on your back, stretch your arms out like being on a cross, have your legs comfortably apart and your toes pointing headward, while stretching your arms out sideways, at the same time stretch your legs downward, keep your toes pointing headward to insure you are stretching your legs properly; while doing this, stretch your back and neck headward; relax and repeat the movement. When doing this movement repeat the Alpha Wave affirmation to yourself (**I am strong in body and keen of mind and my brain is dominated with active Alpha Waves**). Stretch sideways, downwards and headwards all at the same time, farther and farther with each repetition; you want to get to the point where you can do this stretch 10 times before getting out of bed. But start slow, do this stretch 3 times before getting out of bed the first week you start; 6 times your second week; nine times your third week and 10 times your fourth week. By doing this movement lying down it stretches your back, combatting the pull of gravity.

Alpha Stretch

CHAPTER 7

Y ou can lose 3 to 4 inches in height during your lifetime because of the pull of gravity. This movement restores most of your lost natural height by stretching and straightening your spine, tones up most of your muscles, shapes your mind, relaxes you and invigorates you at the same time. You will feel raring to go and prepared for whatever may come your way. All human beings have a internal force of energy that needs to be taken care of and to be trained, because our life depends on it. The generating turbine of energy in human beings is a point approximately 4 centimeters below the naval called Hara. This is the center of gravity in the human body, the flow of human energy nourishes every system of our body and gives us the ability to concentrate. Energy flow connects everything within the human body and this God like force circulates through human energy channels called Meridians. The way human energy flows through the Meridians create a balance that triggers wellness and forms a happy feeling, because · our energy flow reflects our state of mind. The energy Hug creates a most powerful energy massage enabling energy to flow easily through the Meridians, helps to relieve emotional complaints and ailments, such as depression, anxiety, insomnia, self-treatment, preventive health that ·relieves stress related ailments, builds healing energy with physical power that channels the God like force for healing internally, creates a vibratory movement for energy flow helping the body to benefit from the cultivation of this healing energy. Building human energy developing its healing potential and strengthening the flow of this God like force should be a priority of all human beings. So let's learn how to cultivate this God like force and channel it throughout the body.

CHAPTER 8

The energy Hug movement builds energy within your body and is done while lying in bed flat on your back, legs extended normally, cross arms over your chest, left arm over right arm with left hand cupping right shoulder and right hand cupping left shoulder, press shoulders inward and downwards with hands, at the same time firm your chest muscles hard, hold the firming and repeat in your mind the energy Hug affirmation (**I am creating energy within my body that is flowing through my Meridians and energizing every part of my body**); relax and repeat, each time you firm your chest with each succeeding repetition. By the time you reach eight repetitions, you will feel more energy collecting from your adrenal glands that your whole chest will throb with energy, you will have then trapped energy within you and feel raring to go. Do at least 8 repetitions each morning before getting out of bed and the muscles in your chest will feel full of energy; you will feel socially and business ready to lead.

Energy

Hug

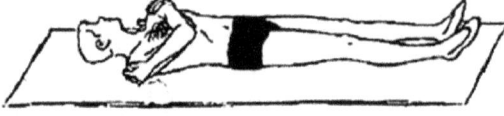

CHAPTER 9

The human body is constructed to exist in a gravitational environment; everything from blood flow to our sense of balance is influenced by the gravitational pull of the earth. There is gravity in everything including the human body. The awareness and perception of our bodies orientation to gravity on earth is attributed in part to the detection of gravity by the Otlith organs or the Utricle and the Saccule, to the detection of the rotational movements by the semicircular canals, both of which are in the inner ear. Gravity sensors in the joints and the touch sensors in the skin are also involved and the eyes contribute by sensing the body's relationship to other objects. Gravity can cause a reduction in the endurance capacity of skeletal muscles; that is why the human body can lose 3 to 4 inches in height during a lifetime due to the pull of gravity. This loss of height can be prevented by balancing the body to gravity. The movement to balance the body to gravity is the Gravity Balancer. The instant pull of gravity on the human body alters our anatomy, our physiology, our mental and psychic responses. Due to the human beings two-legged stance, gravity has altered the human inherited skeletal structure. Most of the stress of gravity on the human body is borne by the intervertebral discs of the balancing spine. These are the 24 small pads of fibrous cartilage which are sandwiched between every pair of your 24 vertebrae. They act as shock absorbers against every strain and stress on the spinal column. The intervertebral discs shrink with age and use. The human being can lose a total of 3 to 4 inches in height during your lifetime. If you could delay the shrinking of your intervertebral discs, you could live longer, look much younger, feel taller and stronger. The movement to delay the shrinking of the intervertebral discs is the Gravity Balancer. This movement is done before getting out bed; lying flat on your back; bend your knees and bring them to your chest, clasp your legs with your arms and raise your hips several inches off the bed; at the same time raise your head slightly off the bed and stretch it away from your body. You will feel a strong pull all the way through your neck and the upper part of your back.

CHAPTER 10

Y ou want to get to the point that you can do this movement 10 times every morning. Start slow, do this movement 3 times every morning the: first week, 6 times the second week, 9 times the third week and 10 times the fourth week. By stretching your whole back and neck, it widens the space between your vertebrae where the intervertebral discs lie. This encourages your shrinking intervertebral discs to stop shrinking and to thicken instead. The nerves in your back will be relieved of much of the compression on your vertebrae and restore the circulation of your organs closer to normal level; you will feel younger, stronger and your concentration power will multiply. Repeat the Gravity Balancer affirmation during each repetition (**My body is balanced to the pull of gravity and it is no longer being deteriorated by the pull of gravity**): There is a direct relationship between our spine and our internal organs. It is important to maintain the spine in optimal condition, keeping the vertebrae aligned will maintain them in optimal position, one on top of another. Research has found that if the spine is aligned every organ in the body operates optimally. To establish spinal alignment, you have to stimulate the spinal column with painless movements of the musculoskeletal system to keep it in postural balance. And Stimulation should be done with a purpose, and the ultimate purpose of any stimulation is to balance the nervous system and allow the body to self-regulate and move in the direction of health. Balancing the nervous system releases the God Force Within; because the internal organs actually determine the health of an individual.

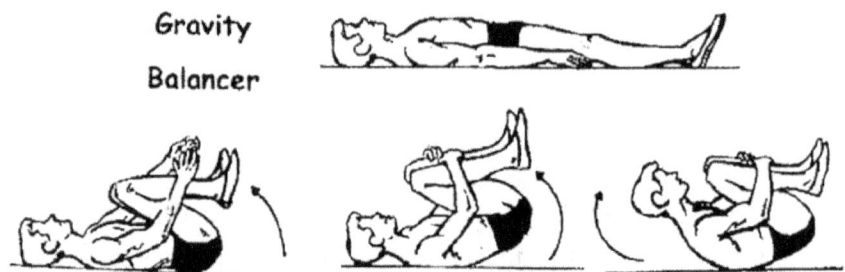

Gravity Balancer

CHAPTER 11

To restore your spinal column's flexibility and relax your back muscles, do · the spine aligner movement. Lie face down, relaxed with your legs straight and heels together; stretch your arms out with palms down; point your toes backwards; keep your arms and knees straight; inhale and raise your arms and legs at the same time; raise your head too at the same time, hold the position as you repeat in your mind the Spine Aligner affirmation (**My spine is strong and aligned and every organ in my body is operating optimally**): then exhale and relax; start slow, do this movement 3 times your first week, 6 times your second week, 9 times your third week and 10 times your fourth week. Do this movement when you wake in the morning, it will stimulate you from head to toe. This movement strengthens the muscles that keep your back straight, with a straight back you feel more confident, more sure of yourself, you think faster and become more creative. This movement helps renormalize the alignments of your different vertebrae. Researchers have found that if you can align the spine and if practiced regularly will keep the spine alignment.

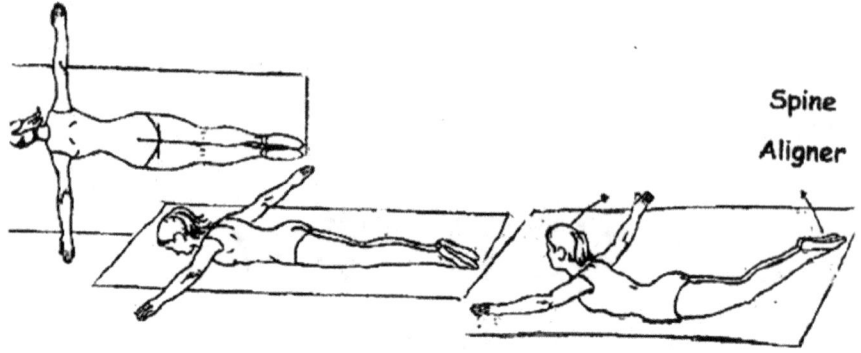

Spine
Aligner

CHAPTER 12

G od is within awaiting us. The question *homo sapiens* need to ask themselves is; are you going to continue to partake of other men sins or are you going to partake of the benefit. The benefit is the Kingdom of God, and you have to believe that the Kingdom of God is within you. Belief alone can create powerful changes in our physiology, but we have to have faith to make those changes permanent. A woman touched the hem of Jesus garment and was healed. Christ explained that her faith had made her whole; belief is often strengthened by an external stimulus and in this guide are the movements you do before getting out of bed to stimulate the inner wisdom that is the body's inner healing ability, resulting in the manifestation of the spirit within.

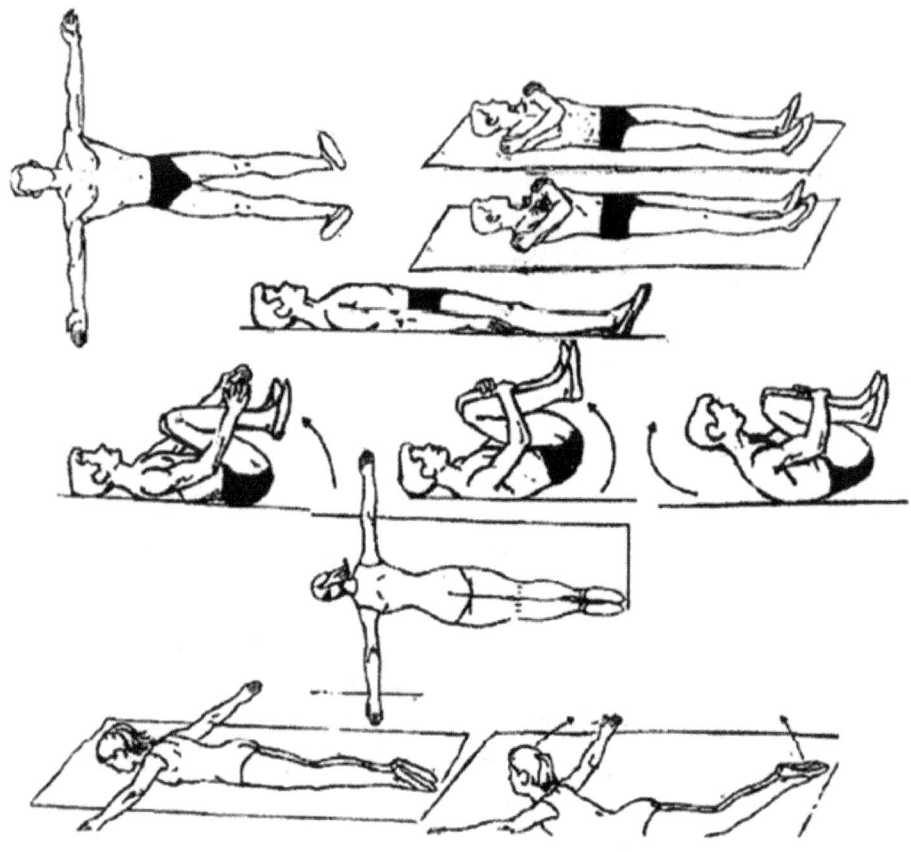

CHAPTER 13

The human being is its own healer. We can make ourselves ill or well, happy or sad, productive or stagnant. To be born human is a miracle and to take advantage of this miracle we as humans have to develop our inner awareness and calm that bounds us to the universe. The first brain wave pattern to be discovered that is associated with being calm, alert and pleasant is the Alpha Wave. Modern Science knows for a fact that kids operate in Alpha up until about eight years old. Silence is the element in which great things fashion themselves. Silence conditions the mind to those sharper illuminations which surely come from God working in your thoughts. Divine guidance is always spoken in a still small voice. The technique is to let yourself down into the relaxed and deep quietness of faith and confidence in clear thinking is possible. Then a sense of direction will be opened to you for dealing with your difficulties. Practice consciously sensing God's presence. Actually, making affirmative statements and holding affirmative thoughts is the first step toward causing the affirmed belief to be actualized. The second step is to put the affirmations into action. To do that act as if the thing affirmed is already true. As you think affirm and act you will strongly tend to feel. Act vigorously and energetically and you will be amazed at the new energy and vigor you will enjoy. Aging is a matter of the spirit, it exists in the imagination before it exists in the body, it is in the mind. Change your image of yourself, see yourself well, of course observing and practicing all the rules of health and you will tend to be that which you visualize and practice. A chief reason that people are beaten down by difficulties is simply that they allow themselves to think they can be beaten. One of the greatest techniques for overcoming difficulty is to learn to believe that they can be overcome and that you can do the overcoming with what God gave you at birth. The human being has a tremendous extension power within themselves. God made you and he never intended that life should defeat you. Say to yourself, God is in me, God is in my whole being. One step that has been found helpful in applying positive attitudes to physical well-being is that of affirmation, the use of positive statements, words are dynamite. If you constantly use negative words concerning your health, you may stimulate negative forces that can adversely affect you. Affirmations have to be wholly positive statements. Properly employed affirmations will improve your health, lengthen your life, rejuvenate your body, increase your happiness, give you success and peace of mind. Put your faith in the thing God has given you the power to reason. One of the greatest of all principles is that humans can do what they think they can do.

"'Believe and Receive"
September 2020
Paul A. Dixon
(434) 401-0395
pad91649@gmail.com

www.ingramcontent.com/pod-product-compliance
Lightning Source LLC
Chambersburg PA
CBHW060358130626
46553CB00003B/1289